SCIENTIFIC MAGIC SERIES

MOLECULES
AND
HEAT
BOOK 3

by Robert Friedhoffer

Magical effect illustrations by Richard Kaufman

All other illustrations by Linda Eisenberg

Photographs by Timothy White

FRANKLIN WATTS
NEW YORK ◆ CHICAGO
LONDON ◆ TORONTO ◆ SYDNEY

To my brother Jeff,
(who even calls me once in a while),
and his entire family: Carol, Elizabeth,
Adam, Randy, and Mark

Library of Congress Cataloging-in-Publication Data

Friedhoffer, Robert.
Molecules and heat / by Robert Friedhoffer ; magic effect
illustrations by Richard Kaufman ; other illustrations by Linda
Eisenberg ; photographs by Timothy White.
p. cm.—(Scientific magic series ; bk. 3)
Includes bibliographical references (p.) and index.
Summary: Experiments, magic tricks, and other activities explore
the scientific principles of molecules and heat.
ISBN 0-531-11053-2
1. Heat—Experiments—Juvenile literature. 2. Molecules—
Experiments—Juvenile literature. [1. Heat—Experiments.
2. Molecules—Experiments. 3. Experiments. 4. Scientific
recreations. 5. Magic tricks.] I. Kaufman, Richard, ill.
II. Eisenberg, Linda, ill. III. White, Timothy, ill. IV. Title.
V. Series: Friedhoffer, Robert. Scientific magic series ; bk. 3.
QC256.F75   1992
536′.078—dc20   92-16960 CIP AC

Printed in the United States of America
6 5 4 3 2 1

CONTENTS

INTRODUCTION 9

MOLECULES 13
Molecules in Rapid Motion 14
    Experiment 1 16
    Experiment 2 17
    Trick 1—The Hypnotic Flower 18
Molecular Action 19
    Experiment 3 20
    Experiment 4 21
Molecular Forces 23
    Experiment 5 25
Characteristics of Solids 26
    Trick 2—The Jumping Rubber Band 26
Characteristics of Liquids 28
    Experiment 6 29
    Trick 3—The Dividing Water 30
    Trick 4—The Floating Disk 32
Capillary Action 34
    Experiment 7 35

HEAT 37
Temperature 38
    Trick 5—The Human Thermometer 39
The Kinetic Theory of Heat 41
The History of the Thermometer 42

The Absolute or Kelvin Scale   45
Everyday Measuring of Temperature   46
Expansion and Contraction of Solids   49
    Betcha 1   52
More Expansion   54
    Experiment 8   56
    Betcha 2   56
Bimetals   59
    Trick 6—The Mental Push 59
Expansion and Contraction of Liquids   60
    Experiment 9   61
Gas Expansion   63
    Trick 7—The Dancing Dime 65
Heat Conduction   66
Household Heat Tips   67
    Betcha 3   69
    Betcha 4   70
    Experiment 10   72
    Experiment 11   72
    Experiment 12   73
Heat Convection   75
    Trick 8—The Power   76
    Trick 9—The Power Revisited 77
    Experiment 13   78
Heat Radiation   79
    Experiment 14   81
    Betcha 5   82
Heat Energy   83
    Experiment 15   83
Calories and Specific Heat   84
    Experiment 16   85
Liquid to Solid   86
    Experiment 17   87
Heat of Fusion and Vaporization   88
    Experiment 18   89
Boiling   90
    Trick 10—Hot-Blooded   91
    Trick 11—The Drinking Bird 94
Regelation   95
    Betcha 6   95

Water Vapor and Weather   96

HEAT ENGINES   98
External Combustion Engines   99
    Experiment 19   100
Internal Combustion Engines   100
Jet and Rocket Engines   102
The Refrigerator   103

SUPPLIERS   105

FOR FURTHER READING   108

INDEX   109

"The whole of science is nothing more than a refinement of everyday thinking."
—Albert Einstein, *Out of My Later Years*

"Science is the best magic."
—Bob Friedhoffer

ACKNOWLEDGMENTS

I would first like to thank Microsoft® Corporation for providing MS Windows™ and MS Word for Windows™ and Logitech, Inc. for providing a Mouseman™ Cordless mouse and a Scanman® Model 256. The aid of these marvelous products lightened the physical chores of writing and were a joy to work with.

I would like to thank the following people for helping make this book possible by supplying ideas, encouragement, and/or inspiration: Sir Isaac Newton, Leibniz, Galileo, Otto van Guericke, John Blake, John Wilkins, René Descartes, David Brewster, Carl Stenquist, Iris Rosoff, Martin Gardner, Peter and Jackie Monticup, the Druckmans, Linda Eisenberg, Lubor Fiedler, Joe Franklin, Lee Freed, Jeff and Eddie at The Funny Store, Martin Gardner, Peter Greenhill, Maria do Rosario Pedreira, Sylvia Hecht, Stephen Baumrin, Andy Helfer and Neal Hollander, Tim White, Richard Kaufman, Howard MacNeil, Alicia Ho White, Constantine "Gus" Philippas, Russel Ward, Laura Hughes, and mon ami Antoine Bruxelles.

INTRODUCTION

Even though this series of six books doesn't have to be read consecutively, it might help the beginning magical scientist to do so. The basics of physics start in the first book. Each succeeding book builds upon the knowledge of the one before. The tricks, experiments, and betchas are in there to help you have fun and get the most that you possibly can out of each book.

When you perform the experiments, you might want to *keep a notebook or diary of all your results*. In keeping the diary, you will be following in the footsteps of such great scientists of the world as Madame Marie Sklodowska Curie (1867–1934)—radiation; Rosalind Elsie Franklin (1920–1958)—DNA; Galileo Galilei (1564–1642)—astronomy, mathematics, and physics; and Albert Einstein (1879–1955)—theoretical physics.

The tricks are laid out with EFFECT first, to let you have an idea of what the trick is about. Next comes the PROPS section, so you'll know what "stuff" you need. Then comes the METHOD, or ROU-

TINE part, which fully explains the workings of the trick. The NOTES that are at the very end of the trick try to tie the scientific principle in with the routine.

If you want to teach the science behind the tricks, you might want to explain the workings of the experiments to your friends. If you want to be a magician, you're better off not telling your friends how the tricks work. If your friends know the secrets to the trick, there is no magic.

To become a magician, you need to know all of the secrets of magic. To learn many of the secrets, you have to know something about science. You'll learn many of the "secrets" of science in this series of books.

When you learn the science, you become the magician. You just have to learn how to present the scientific principle in a mystifying way.

If you have any science tricks of your own that you think you would like to share with others, please send them along to me in care of my publisher:

FRANKLIN WATTS
95 Madison Avenue
New York, New York 10016

Perhaps I'll have room to place your trick with your name next to it in my next science/magic book. Study hard and work hard, and the universe can be yours.

Bob Friedhoffer

AN OPEN LETTER TO ALL WHO READ THIS BOOK

Greetings!

Physics—the study of matter and energy and how they affect each other—is all around us! Pretty scary thought, eh?

It's not really. Physics doesn't have to be frightening at all. There's little that we do everyday that doesn't involve physics.

Here's a list of some things that use physics: riding skateboards and bicycles, playing video games, watching TV, listening to stereos, baking a cake, cooking an egg, drawing pictures, driving a car, working on your computer, shooting an arrow, playing the piano or guitar, turning on your shower, doing magic tricks, and playing practical jokes. In other words, physics is everywhere, and it can be fun if you look at it with an open mind.

I've written this series with as light a touch as possible. I've put in very little math, and all of the EXPERIMENTS can be done at or near your home for practically no expense. Almost all of the magic tricks are done with stuff you find around the house.

When you perform the magic, remember that if you want to fool your friends, you should keep the secret to yourself. If someone wants to know, "How did you do that trick?" you can honestly say, "I did it with science—physics, to be exact."

If you wish to share any secrets with your friends, don't tell them how the tricks are done; let them read the book. They can buy it or take it out of the library. If you tell them how you do a trick and they don't have to put any effort into finding out the secret, they won't respect you or the trick.

I hope that you enjoy the books in this series, and all of the experiments, tricks, and betchas that you'll find inside.

NOTE: About the use of the metric system and English system in this book. Although the metric system is easier to use, both systems are used in this series of books. In some experiments and tricks, only metric measurements are used; in others, only the English system. In still others, both are given.

Bob Friedhoffer
aka The Madman of Magic

MOLECULES

Over 2,400 years ago, the Greek philosopher Democritus (di MOK reh tus) reasoned that all matter
could be divided into smaller and smaller pieces,
until only one small piece of that matter was left. This
indivisible part of matter was called an *atom*.

Some of the other philosophers of the day
thought that you could divide matter in half, then

half again, then half again, forever into smaller and smaller pieces, without ever coming to the smallest piece. No matter how small you made a piece, you could divide it in half again. That would mean there would be an infinite number of pieces.

In the days of Democritus, scientists did not test their theories in laboratory experiments. However, day-to-day observations could be explained by the fact that matter was not continuous as it seemed to be, but was, in fact, many tiny specks that just gave the appearance of one large piece of matter. With today's scanning electron microscopes, we can actually see images of individual atoms.

Using just the power of his mind, and no laboratory methods, Democritus was able to come up with a theory that would not be proved correct for over 2,000 years.

Today we know that the smallest piece of matter that can have a separate existence is the *molecule*. Molecules are made up of atoms. A molecule of H_2O (water) is made up of two hydrogen atoms and one oxygen atom. It is possible to break the molecule

apart into three separate pieces, one atom of oxygen and two separate atoms of hydrogen, but then we would not have water. We would have two separate gases. The original material will have lost its waterlike qualities.

MOLECULES IN RAPID MOTION

In 1827, a botanist by the name of Robert Brown was looking through a microscope. He saw that

**The atomium in Brussels, Belgium, is a
giant model of an iron atom. Eight
electrons surround the nucleus.**

some small particles of solid matter suspended in a drop of water were bouncing around inside the drop of water in a crazy pattern, almost as though they were dancers moving to the beat of the latest tune.

In 1863, it was suggested that the solid particles were getting knocked around by molecules of water.

We call this movement *Brownian motion*. It turns out that molecules of all matter are constantly in motion.

Brownian motion can be observed through a microscope.

Experiment 1

Do this experiment ONLY with adult permission and help.

APPARATUS
    towels
    a candle
    a candle holder
    matches
    a glass jar
    a magnifying glass

PROCEDURE
1. Close the door and windows in a room. Stuff towels at the bottom edge of the door to prevent any air from coming in.

2. Put the candle in the candle holder and place it in the middle of a table, away from anything else that can burn.

3. Light the candle. **(Be careful when you do this so you don't burn yourself or start a fire.)** Let it burn for a few seconds, and then blow it out. You will see smoke rise from the candle's wick. The smoke is composed of particles of ash, suspended in air.

4. Observe the smoke. What happens to it? The smoke doesn't stick together in a clump. It starts to spread out because the molecules of air are constantly bombarding the pieces of ash that make up the smoke, forcing them to move about the room.

5. When you try this experiment, capture some of the smoke in a clean, empty glass jar. Try to examine some of the captured smoke under a strong magnifying glass. You might actually see the particles of ash getting knocked about by air molecules.

Experiment 2
APPARATUS
    a glass full of water
    food coloring or fountain pen ink

PROCEDURE
1. Place the water-filled glass on a vibration-free surface.
2. Gently place one drop of food coloring or ink on the center of the water's surface.

3. Leave the glass alone and come back at two-hour intervals to see what happens.

After a little while, the food coloring starts to spread throughout the glass. You are observing the same thing that Robert Brown observed more than 160 years ago. The molecular action of the water is spreading the food coloring or ink around.

Trick 1
The Hypnotic Flower

EFFECT: You "hypnotize" a volunteer and make her think that she smells a beautiful flower.

PROPS

a small rubber bulb.

a 3-foot length of plastic tubing (⅛-inch inside diameter)

a bottle of sweet-smelling perfume

NOTE: The rubber bulb and tubing can be found in a magic/novelty shop or mail order catalog that sells practical jokes under the name of "the squirting flower" or "the plate lifter."

SETUP
1. Partially fill the rubber bulb with a small amount of perfume. Attach the tubing to the bulb.
2. Run the tubing down your shirtsleeve and secure it under your watchband or under a rubber band. Let the bulb end of the tube hang inside your shirt, in a position that allows your arm or elbow to squeeze it.

ROUTINE

"I'm going to hypnotize you, so you will think of beautiful flowers. I'm going to do such a good job that you'll be able to smell them."

Start to make hypnotic gestures toward your helper and say things like, "You're getting tired. Your eyes are getting heavy. In just a moment you will be smelling the most beautiful rose in the world."

At this point, you point your hands at her face and gently squeeze the bulb with your arm or elbow. A little bit of perfume should arrive at the end of the tube, and in a moment or two, your subject will be able to smell it.

NOTE: Brownian motion and air currents will force the aroma of the perfume to spread into the room from the opening in the tube's end. The molecules of air, a gas, are in constant motion, and they will knock the molecules of perfume around, spreading them throughout the room. When you press the bulb, you increase the pressure inside of it. The perfume rushes out of the bulb into the tube, increasing the pressure in the tube. The pressure in the tube forces some of the gas into the room. Brownian motion does the rest.

MOLECULAR ACTION, OR THE KINETIC THEORY OF MATTER

The kinetic theory of matter states that all matter is made of particles whose motion determines whether the matter is solid, liquid, or gas.

A *solid* has a definite shape and a definite volume.

The molecules of a solid are close together in a "crystalline structure." That means that the molecules are in a generally fixed position in a "typical" arrangement.

The molecular motion of a solid is limited to vibration. If heat is applied to the molecules of solids, they start to vibrate rapidly. If enough heat is applied, the molecules break away from the crystalline structure. When that happens, the solid melts. When a solid melts, it turns into a liquid.

Experiment 3
APPARATUS
    a chocolate bar

PROCEDURE
Wash your hands, and then hold an unwrapped chocolate bar in your hand. What happens? (Your mouth probably starts to water, but that's psychology and not part of physics.)

The chocolate starts to get mushy and then turns into a liquid. The molecular "bonds" started to break down when your hand added heat to the chocolate. The chocolate molecules started to move about more rapidly and turn into a messy liquid. You may now lick all of the chocolate from your hand and eat any that didn't melt.

See how physics can be fun. Next time you have melted chocolate on your hand, and your mom yells at you, just tell her that you're doing a science experiment. She may even believe you.

A *liquid* has a definite volume, but no definite shape.
The molecules of a liquid are farther apart than those of a solid. The molecules are not arranged in a crystalline structure like those in a solid. In liquids, the molecules can move over each other, sliding all around, but they are still fairly close together. The molecular motion is generally limited to movement within the liquid itself.

When heat is added to a liquid, the molecules start to move faster. They knock into each other at a faster and faster rate. If one of these fast-moving molecules gets near the surface of the liquid, it may escape from the liquid. This is called *evaporation*. The individual molecules that leave the liquid form a *vapor*. A vapor, like a gas, has no definite shape and no definite volume.

Experiment 4
APPARATUS
> a cake pan, or large, flat container
> a grease pencil or crayon

PROCEDURE

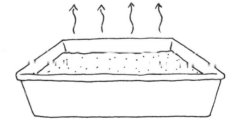

**Water evaporating
from a cake pan**

1. Fill the container or cake pan with water. Mark the level of the water with the crayon or grease pencil.

2. Place the container in the corner of a room in an out-of-the-way place so no one disturbs it. Examine the pan every twelve hours. What happens to the water in the pan?

The amount of water decreases. The water in the pan has absorbed some of the heat in the room. The molecules of the water started to move around faster and faster and eventually some left the liquid water as water vapor.

Sometimes solids can evaporate without going through the liquid state. A good example of this is seen with mothballs. The volume of the mothball diminishes, but you'll never see a liquid. The mothball transforms from the solid state to the gas state without becoming a liquid. The change of state from solid to gas without becoming a liquid is called *sublimation*.

A *gas* has no definite shape and no definite volume.

In general, the molecules of a gas are always in rapid motion, even when they are in a container. An enormous amount of gas molecules bombard the container's walls every second. This constant bom-

Gas molecules flitting around a container

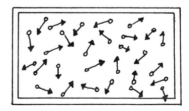

bardment acts as a steady push against the container's walls. If the molecules are forced into a container with a smaller volume, or more gas is pushed into the same container, the molecules smash into the container's walls even more frequently.

The kinetic theory of matter represents a gas as a bunch of rapidly moving molecules, always smacking into the walls of the container and each other. The molecules never stop moving and never lie peacefully on the bottom of their container. Scientists have figured out that, at sea level and a temperature of 0° Celsius (32° Fahrenheit), the average oxygen molecule makes about 5 billion (5×10^8 or 5,000,000,000) collisions every second and has an average speed of .3333 (⅓) of a mile per second.

MOLECULAR FORCES

When molecules are close to each other in solids and liquids, they usually clump together. This clumping together is called *cohesion*. Cohesion is especially strong in solids, where the molecules are in very close contact. When cohesion is at work, it is very hard to break the molecular bonds by pulling a solid apart.

This resistance to being pulled apart is called *tensile strength*, or *tenacity*. It takes many pounds of pressure to pull apart an iron bar. Iron has a relatively high tensile strength.

An iron bar has high tensile strength.

If you manage to break a solid into two pieces and then try to put the two pieces back together as one by placing them next to each other, you won't be able to get the molecules close enough together for cohesion to work. To get the molecules close enough for cohesion, you have to heat both pieces and weld them together. If you use a little heat to melt the edges of a broken chocolate bar and then push them together, they will stay together when the chocolate is allowed to cool.

To get an iron bar back together after it has been pulled apart or broken, a blacksmith will first heat the broken ends, place one on top of the other, and then hammer them. Without hammering, molec-

ular bonding will not occur. The high tensile strength of steel (an alloy of iron and other metals) makes it a perfect material to use for the frameworks of large structures like bridges and office buildings.

Experiment 5

APPARATUS

a newspaper

PROCEDURE

1. Take a sheet of newspaper and cut a 1-inch-wide strip from it. Hold the strip at both ends and try to pull it apart. What happens?
2. Take the remaining piece of paper and twist it into a long ropelike strand. Hold the strand at both ends and try to pull it apart. What happens?

3. Wet the middle of the strand with water. What happens?

EXPLANATION: The 1-inch strip of newspaper has little tensile strength and rips apart easily. The rope-like strand of paper has a much greater tensile strength, and you are probably unable to pull it apart. When you wet the middle of the paper, the molecular bonds between the strands of paper are weakened, giving the paper less tensile strength, so it becomes easier to pull it apart.

CHARACTERISTICS OF SOLIDS

When a material returns to its original shape after being bent or distorted in any other way, it exhibits *elasticity*. This property is very useful in springs, rubber bands, bows for archery, and the elastic tops of underwear.

**Elasticity is useful
to help hold up your
underwear and socks.**

Trick 2
The Jumping Rubber Band
EFFECT: You place a rubber band around your index and middle fingers and it magically jumps to the ring finger and pinky.

PROPS
  a rubber band

ROUTINE
Place the rubber band around your fingers, as displayed in the drawings. When you straighten out your first two fingers, the band appears to jump onto the last two fingers.

NOTE: The rubber band has elasticity. When you stretch it out of shape and hold it under pressure, it comes back to its original shape when pressure is released.

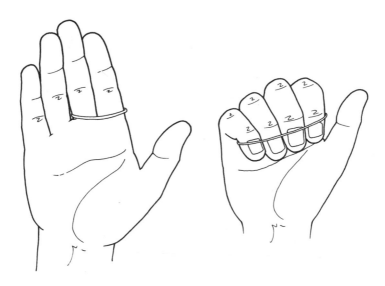

**Extend the fingers of your right hand
straight out and place the rubber
band around the base of the index
and middle fingers.**
**Take the loop on the palm side of your
hand and stretch it, so that you can
place all four fingers inside of it
when you bend them, just as pictured
above. Show your friends the back of
your hand and they will see the loop
around the first and second fingers.
Straighten your fingers out, keeping
them next to one another, and the
rubber band, when seen from the back
of your hand, will appear to jump to
the ring finger and pinky.**

The opposite of elasticity is *plasticity*. When an object is bent or deformed and it doesn't come back to its original shape, but stays in the shape that you bent or molded it, it is said to be plastic. (**NOTE:** In science, if we say something is plastic, we are talking of the above feature: that something is capable of being molded. We do not mean the material, plastic, that is used to make ballpoint pens, toys, and fast-food containers.)

Clay, Play-Doh®, and candle wax are all examples of materials that exhibit plasticity.

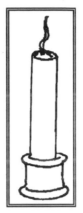

Some metals, such as gold, silver, aluminum, and copper, can be beaten by hammers or pressed between very powerful rollers into very thin sheets. Gold can be beaten or rolled into sheets that are so thin, about 1/50,000 of an inch, that you can actually see light through them. Gold and the other metals that can be changed this way are said to be *malleable*.

An example of a malleable metal that you have around the house is aluminum foil. The foil probably started out as a large ingot (a block or bar of metal) that was shaped and formed and eventually rolled out into a thin sheet. The thin sheets may then be formed or molded into various shapes.

Metals such as gold, silver, platinum, and copper can be pulled through a die into very thin wires. When they can be transformed like that they are said to be *ductile*.

The *hardness* of a material is measured by its capacity to scratch other materials. The Mohs' scale shows the hardness of different minerals. Number 1 is the softest, number 15 is the hardest.

Mohs' Scale		
1-talc	6-orthoclase	11-fused zirconium
2-gypsum	7-vitreous silica	oxide
3-calcite	8-quartz	12-fused alumina
4-fluorite	9-topaz	13-silicon carbide
5-apatite	10-garnet	14-boron carbide
		15-diamond

CHARACTERISTICS OF LIQUIDS

When a liquid has a free surface, not touching its container, cohesive force (cohesion) makes it act as though it were covered by a skin. This behavior is called *surface tension.*

Experiment 6
APPARATUS
    a clear, clean water glass
    water

PROCEDURE
1. Fill the glass halfway with water.
2. Look through the sides of the glass and you will notice that the water at the sides is a little bit higher than the rest of the water's surface. The water molecules, being attracted to the glass, "wet" the glass and curve upward because of cohesion.

Surface tension causes the water to bend up at the edges in the half-filled glass and to bend down in the overfilled glass.

3. Carefully fill the glass completely with water. Slowly add as much water to the top as possible. Now examine the water surface. What do you see?

    When you fill the water to a level exactly even with the top of the glass and then add just a little bit more, you can see the water bulging upward, above the sides of the glass.

EXPLANATION: Molecules of water are pulled down by the molecules beneath them, up by the molecules above them, and sideways by the molecules next to them. There are no molecules above the ones on the surface to supply an upward pull. This causes the water to act as though a skin is on the surface. This "skin" is what we call surface tension. Surface tension allows bubbles and foam to form on top of liquids, makes drops of water round, and allows bugs to skim across the surface of a pond.

Trick 3
The Dividing Water

Do this trick ONLY with adult supervision.

EFFECT: A puddle of water is divided, something like Moses and the Red Sea.

PROPS
    a clean, grease-free, serving tray
    a cup of water
    a small glass
    ¼ ounce of denatured alcohol (bought at a hardware or paint store) **Be careful—this stuff is poisonous**

SETUP
Pour enough water into the tray to form a small puddle on the bottom. Put the alcohol in a small glass. As far as the audience is concerned, the alcohol is water.

DO NOT DRINK THE ALCOHOL and DO NOT LET ANYONE ELSE DRINK IT. DENATURED ALCOHOL IS A POISON.

ROUTINE
Bring out the tray of water and put it on a table. You may talk about Moses and the Red Sea (EXODUS 14:21) and the parting of the Red Sea to escape from the Egyptians. Tell your audience that the parting of the Red Sea was a miracle, but you have figured out a way to demonstrate what it might have looked like.

"According to the Bible, Moses spread his arm out and the Red Sea parted. Watch carefully as I pour just a little bit of water on this puddle."

Pour the alcohol onto the middle of the puddle, and you and your audience will see the most amazing thing. The water starts to shimmer and in just a moment it separates, leaving a clear, dry area on the bottom of the tray.

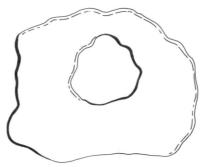

AS SOON AS YOU ARE FINISHED WITH THIS TRICK, POUR THE WATER FROM THE TRAY DOWN THE DRAIN AND WASH THE SMALL GLASS OUT THOROUGHLY.

NOTE: The alcohol weakens the surface tension, cohesive force, of the water at the point where it is placed. The cohesive force of the other water molecules, untouched by the alcohol, pulls the water back, leaving the dry spot on the bottom of the tray.

Trick 4
The Floating Disk
EFFECT: You ask your friends to try to float a half-dollar coin on the surface of a glass of water, and they are unable to do so. You take the coin and manage to successfully float it.

PROPS
    a highly polished half-dollar
    a fake half-dollar, made by pressing a disc of

aluminum foil onto the half-dollar and molding it (the foil is malleable) until it looks just like a half-dollar
    a glass full of water
    a fork

SETUP

Sit at the table where you will perform this trick. Place the real half-dollar on one side of your lap and the fake half-dollar on the other side. Put the glass of water on the table. Put the fork on your lap, next to the fake coin.

ROUTINE
Ask your friends if they can float the half-dollar on the surface of the water. They will try to do it, but will be unable to do so. It will sink to the bottom of the glass.

Take the half-dollar back and reach into your lap to pick up the fork. As you reach for the fork, drop the real coin in your lap and pick up the fake one. Hold it gently, as it is very fragile.

Place the fake coin on the fork, and gently lower the fork to the surface of the water. The flat, aluminum foil coin will rest on the water's surface, supported by surface tension. Take the coin out of the water by placing the fork underneath and lifting both fork and coin out of the glass. Put them both in your lap.

Leaving the fake coin and fork in your lap, bring up the real coin and ask your friends if they would like to try to float it again. They will probably say that they would like to use the fork, so once again go to your lap to retrieve it. Naturally, they will be unable to do the trick.

The force of gravity is less than the force of surface tension with the fake coin. The force of gravity is greater than surface tension with the real coin.

CAPILLARY ACTION

Water seeks its own level because of the equalizing effect of the gravity on each water molecule. There is one case where this does not hold true.

If a very narrow glass or plastic tube is placed in some liquids, water in particular, the liquid rises in the tube, just like magic. But, this isn't magic, it's *capillary action*. When the narrow tube is placed in the liquid, the force of surface tension is greater than gravity. The water is attracted to the walls of the tube. As you saw in Experiment 6, the water curves up where it touches the glass walls. Surface tension

Capillary action causes the liquid to rise higher in the narrower tube than in the wider tube.

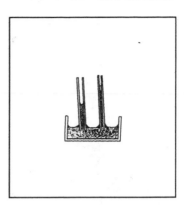

pulls the "skin" of water tight. As a result, the water actually climbs the walls of the tube. The thinner the tube, the higher the liquid will climb.

When the pull of gravity equals the surface tension of the liquid in the tube, the maximum height is reached. In a tube that's 1/32 inch in diameter, the water can pull itself up to a height of at least 3½ inches. Capillary action is used to help test liquids. The small tube is placed in the liquid, the liquid rises, the tube is pulled out, and the liquid is forced out by air pressure onto an examining instrument. Doctors use capillary action to get blood samples from a small pinprick on your finger.

Experiment 7
APPARATUS
    a glass of water
    a strip of paper toweling, 1-inch wide
    a serving tray

**Paper towels will absorb water
through capillary action.**

PROCEDURE

Place the glass on the tray. Put the paper towel halfway into the water. Examine the paper towel at five-minute intervals. What do you see?

As time passes, the portion of towel that is not in the water gets wet. Capillary action has drawn the water out of the glass and onto the dry parts of the paper.

HEAT

Without heat, life as we know it, could not exist. In addition to being a necessity of life, heat is a useful tool to humankind. Heat is a necessity for chemical reactions. We use heat to cook, keep warm, iron our clothes, run automobiles, and lots more things. Can you make a list of fifteen uses of heat?

Up until about one hundred years ago, people thought that heat was a fluid—a substance without

weight that could not be seen, but could be passed from one body or object to another. They also thought the same thing of cold. These people were mistaken. In the next few pages, you're going to learn more about heat than you ever thought existed, and you'll have a good time doing it.

TEMPERATURE

Temperature is a measure of the intensity of heat, not the quantity of heat. Way back in prehistoric days there were no thermometers. Temperature was determined by how hot or cold someone felt. That's okay if you live all by yourself: when you're cold, you turn up the heat or put on a sweater; when you're hot, you turn on the air conditioner or put on shorts. There can be many reasons why you feel hot when I feel cold. You can be dressed warmer, maybe one of us is sick, or maybe our perception of heat is different.

People perceive temperature in different ways.

2 JOKES

"It was so hot yesterday, that I saw a dog chasing a cat, and they were both walking."

"It was so cold last winter that people had to put things in the refrigerator to keep them warm."

Trick 5
The Human Thermometer

EFFECT: You control a spectator's mind by confusing her sense of hot and cold.

PROPS

3 bowls of water: one warm, one cold, one lukewarm

(**NOTE:** Do not use hot water.); label each bowl appropriately—"Warm," "Cold," "Lukewarm"

a blindfold
a towel to dry your assistant's hands

ROUTINE

Bring out three bowls of water: one warm, one cold, one lukewarm. They are marked to show which is which. Ask for a volunteer assistant, and say, "I am now going to show the power that I have over the minds of ordinary people. You see before you three bowls of water: one warm, one cold, and one lukewarm. Please place your hand in each bowl and verify that they are as I stated."

COLD　　　　LUKEWARM　　　　WARM

She verifies this, then you continue.

"I will now blindfold you. Do not worry; I will do nothing to embarrass you. (Don't do anything silly to embarrass her.) At this point, I will place your hand in a bowl, and I want you to tell the rest of the audience which bowl it is."

First, place her hand in the lukewarm bowl. "Which one is this?"

When she answers properly, place it in the cold bowl. "Which one is this?"

When she answers properly, leave her hand in the cold bowl for a moment and say, "I will now use my powers to cloud your perception and confuse you."

Move your hands over her head in a mystical way, then take her hand from the cold bowl and place it in the lukewarm bowl, saying, "Which bowl is this?"

Surprisingly, she should say it is the bowl of warm water.

Take her hand from the lukewarm bowl. Then place her *other* hand first in the cold bowl, and then in the warm. Have her identify each bowl, which she should be able to do with no problem. Now say, "I will now cloud your mind once again."

First, place the last hand she used in the warm bowl for a moment and have her identify the bowl. Next, place her hand in the lukewarm bowl and ask her to identify the bowl. She will say the cold bowl of water.

METHOD: The trick is self-working. The human body can play tricks on itself.

Try this before you perform the trick on someone. Fill the three bowls of water as stated above. Place one hand in the warm water, and one hand in the cold. Next put both hands together into the middle bowl. You'll find that the hand that was in the cold water will feel as though it's in the warm, and that the hand that was in the warm water feels as though it's in the cold.

Our body can confuse itself. That's one reason why we need a better way, like a thermometer, to tell the temperature than just using our feelings.

THE KINETIC THEORY OF HEAT

The kinetic theory of heat was developed by two British scientists, Count von Rumford (1753–1814) and James Prescott Joule (1818–1889). The theory states that heat is the motion of molecules. When an object is warm, its molecules move rapidly; when it's cool, the molecules move slowly. The cooler the object, the less rapid the motion of the molecules. In 1798 Rumford was boring cannon barrels and noticed that the amount of heat generated kept increasing as long as the boring continued. At this time, heat was considered matter, an invisible fluid. Rumford realized that heat was the direct result of

mechanical motion—in this case drilling—and not a separate form of matter.

Joule was a physicist who developed experiments to prove that heat had a mechanical equivalent, that a fixed amount of work equaled a fixed amount of heat.

4.18 *joules* (named in honor of Joule) equals 1 *calorie*. A calorie is the amount of heat needed to raise the temperature of 1 gram of water 1 degree Celsius.

THE HISTORY OF THE THERMOMETER

In general, with few exceptions, when things are heated they expand or get bigger; when they are cooled, they shrink in size. Thermometers (from the Greek meaning "heat measure") use the fact that things expand when heated and contract when cooled to show changes in temperature.

In 1603 Galileo Galilei (1564–1642) invented the thermometer. The thermometer was a long tube with an attached bulb. Galileo warmed the air in the tube by warming the bulb, then placed the open end of the tube in a bucket of water. When the bulb cooled, the air in the bulb contracted, a minor vacuum formed, and water was drawn up into the tube.

**A modern version
of Galileo's
thermometer**

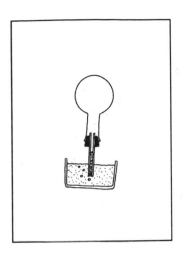

When air temperature rose, the air in the bulb expanded, forcing water out of the tube. When the temperature fell, the air in the tube contracted and water was drawn further up the tube.

The water level in the tube indicated the temperature. The problem with this style of thermometer is that air pressure also affects the level of water in the tube and in the bucket.

Ferdinand II de' Medici (1610–1670), an Italian experimenter, developed the sealed glass tube thermometer in 1654, using alcohol and water. The problem with this thermometer was that it was inaccurate at very low and very high temperatures. The water froze at 0° Celsius (32° Fahrenheit) and the alcohol boiled at a temperature well below that needed to boil water.

In 1699, Guillaume Amontons (1663–1705), a French physicist, invented a gas thermometer based on the change of gas pressure rather than gas volume, using mercury instead of water or alcohol. He was the first to show that water always boiled at the same temperature, even though he didn't have a numerical value for that temperature.

In 1714, a German physicist, Daniel Gabriel Fahrenheit (1686–1736), used mercury as the fluid in a glass tube thermometer, combining the ideas of de' Medici and Amontons. Mercury's freezing point is quite low and its boiling point is quite high, and, therefore, mercury is well suited for measuring temperatures.

There are many stories about Fahrenheit's use of 32° as the freezing point of water. No one is sure which story is true. One of the stories is that Fahrenheit noted that the lowest point he could get on the thermometer was from a mixture of water, ice, and ammonium chloride. He called that point "zero." He decided that a water and ice mixture should be 32°, that human body temperature should be 100° (incorrectly), and computed that water boiled at 212°. The important part of Fahrenheit's work is that he developed a standardized scale to measure temperature.

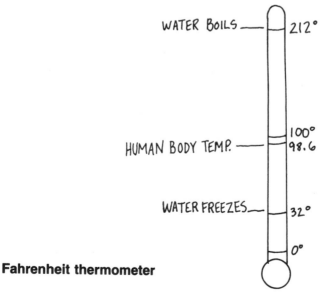

Fahrenheit thermometer

Celsius thermometer

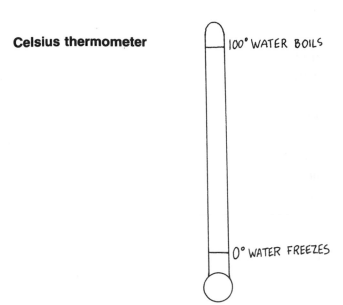

100° WATER BOILS

0° WATER FREEZES

Twenty-eight years after Fahrenheit, in 1742, Anders Celsius (1701-1744), the Swedish astronomer, suggested that a more uniform scale be adopted for measuring temperature. Thirty-two degrees was a strange number to use for a constant starting point. Celsius thought that 0° for the freezing point made a lot more sense. At any temperature below 0°, water would be a solid; at any temperature above, it would be a liquid or gas.

Celsius also suggested that 100 be the number assigned to the point that water boils and turns into a gas. This was called the Centigrade (Latin for "100 steps") scale for 206 years. In 1948, an international agreement was reached changing the name to the Celsius scale, in honor of its inventor.

THE ABSOLUTE OR KELVIN SCALE

In 1848, the British physicist, William Thomson (1824–1907), who later became Lord Kelvin, suggested that the lowest of all possible temperatures in the universe be −273.16° Celsius. His research showed that for every degree that a gas was cooled below 0° Celsius, the gas would shrink by $\frac{1}{273}$. This also meant that the energy of the gas molecules declined by $\frac{1}{273}$, and at −273.16° Celsius all movement of all gas molecules would stop. He invented a new temperature scale called the absolute system.

   −273.16° Celsius was called absolute zero; −273.16° Celsius equals −459.69° on the Fahrenheit scale.

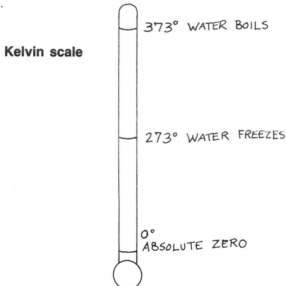

Kelvin scale

373° WATER BOILS

273° WATER FREEZES

0°
ABSOLUTE ZERO

EVERYDAY MEASURING OF TEMPERATURE

The average thermometer that you'll find at home is a long glass tube with a small glass bulb at the bottom. Inside this glass tube is a liquid, usually alcohol, that expands and contracts with changes in temperature. As it gets hotter and expands, the fluid is forced up the narrow tube. As it gets colder and contracts, the fluid is pulled back into the bulb.

A modern home thermometer can usually measure on the Fahrenheit and Celsius scales.

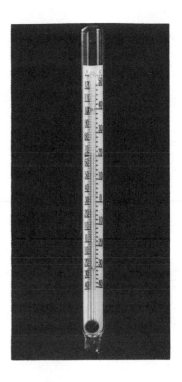

In order to have an accurate measure of temperature, we must be able to determine certain points on the thermometer. This determination of certain points, a standardized, uniform scale, is the major importance of Fahrenheit's work.

As stated above in the history of the thermometer, there are two good points of reference that never change at sea level. They are the freezing point and the boiling point of water. When we place a thermometer in a mixture of pure water and ice, we find that the temperature indicated (the freezing point) will always be the same. The same holds true when we hold the thermometer in boiling water.

There are three generally accepted systems for measuring temperature.

	FAHRENHEIT SCALE (everyday usage)	THE CELSIUS SCALE (formerly centigrade)	THE KELVIN SCALE (scientific)
	U.S.A.	*Rest of world*	*Based on Celsius*
Absolute zero	−459.69°	−273.16°	0°
Freezing	32°	0°	273°
Boiling	212°	100°	373°

If you would like to do a little bit of math, you can change back and forth from Celsius to Fahrenheit with the formula:

$$\text{Fahrenheit} = \tfrac{9}{5}\,C + 32$$

or

$$\text{Celsius} = \tfrac{5}{9}\,F - 32$$

A little poem to help you remember the approximate difference between Celsius and Fahrenheit is:

CELSIUS
Thirty is hot . . .
Twenty is nice . . .
Ten is cold . . .
And Zero is ice.

If you wanted to convert those Celsius temperatures to Fahrenheit, you'd find out that:

$$30° \text{ Celsius} = 86° \text{ Fahrenheit}$$

$$\frac{9}{5} \times \frac{30}{1} = \frac{270}{5} = 54 \qquad 54 + 32 = 86$$

$$20° \text{ Celsius} = 68° \text{ Fahrenheit}$$
$$10° \text{ Celsius} = 50° \text{ Fahrenheit}$$

$$\frac{9}{5} \times \frac{10}{1} = \frac{90}{5} = 18 \qquad 18 + 32 = 50$$

$$0° \text{ Celsius} = 32° \text{ Fahrenheit}$$

EXPANSION AND CONTRACTION OF SOLIDS

The kinetic theory tells us that when a body is heated, its molecules start to move faster and knock into adjoining molecules more vigorously than before. Because of this action, the molecules spread out, moving farther apart. The volume of the body increases because the molecules are farther apart. Gases usually expand more than liquids and liquids usually expand more than solids.

It has been discovered that most solids expand a definite amount for every degree of temperature that they are raised. That means that a given volume of iron, copper, aluminum, or zinc, in fact almost every solid, will always expand the same amount as it is raised through a set temperature range.

A Russian teacher and author by the name of Yakov Perelman (1882–1942) told a cute story. He said that the telephone lines between Moscow and Leningrad do a vanishing act, as though they were stolen. Every winter, 500 meters of these lines vanish without a trace. However, no one ever worried. Every summer, the vanished telephone lines returned.

What Perelman meant was that because of the contraction of the copper wires, the amount of wire, when measured in the winter, was 500 meters less than when measured in the summer.

During the winter of 1927 the steel framework of a bridge over the river Seine in Paris, France, contracted because of the cold. As the steel contracted, the paving stones on the bridge were forced out and the bridge had to be closed to traffic.

The amount of expansion for many solids has been measured. The measurement is given as the *coefficients of linear expansion*. This sounds pretty complicated, but all it means is that different things expand at different rates. The "coefficient" simply means how much each item expands for each unit of length for each degree Celsius that the temperature rises. Some of these numbers are given in the chart below.

Coefficients of Linear Expansion	
Aluminum	0.000024
Brass	0.000019
Copper	0.000017
Glass (plate)	0.000009
Glass (Pyrex)	0.0000036
Ice	0.000051
Iron	0.000011
Lead	0.000029
Silver	0.000017

These numbers seem very small, but can add up rather quickly. On very hot days, railroad tracks can expand so much that they get warped and twisted up so badly that trains can't run on them. Here's an example of how train tracks may get messed up by high temperatures.

In the desert, the temperatures can range from a low of below freezing, 0° Celsius (32° F), at night to a high of 50° Celsius (122° F) during the afternoon. This is a difference of 50° C. Railroad tracks are composed mostly of iron. The coefficient of linear expansion for iron is 0.000011. To find out how much 1000 meters (1,094 yards) of track increases in length from the nighttime low temperature to the day-time high temperature, we multiply 1000 meters by the difference in temperature in Celsius, 50, by the coefficient for iron .000011.

$$1000 \times 50 = 50,000$$
$$50,000 \times .000011 = 0.55 \text{ meters (0.6017 yards)}$$

For every 1,000 meters of track that you measure at night, there is an extra .55 meters (about 1.8 feet) during the daytime.

Sometimes road surfaces get so hot that they expand and buckle (bulge and crinkle) so much that they can't be driven upon by wheeled vehicles.

When roads, sidewalks, bridges, and other structures, as well as machines, are designed, expansion is considered. That's why you will find expansion joints (the stuff between concrete blocks) in roadways and sidewalks, rollers and rockers at the ends of bridges, and piston rings inside of auto-mobile engines.

You may have noticed that when you turn on a hot water faucet, after a few moments the amount of

Expansion and contraction, caused by heat differentials, can make bridges collapse.

Heat can cause roadways to buckle and crack.

water coming out of the faucet slows down. I used to think that someone else in the house had opened up a faucet and taken some of my hot water. I found out that I was wrong. As the hot water runs through the plumbing pipes, faucet, and washers, everything gets heated up. As they get heated up, they start to expand. As the parts of the faucet expand at different rates, the water flow gets constricted, so less water comes out.

Betcha 1

> **DO THIS ONLY WITH THE PERMISSION AND HELP OF AN ADULT.**

Attach a 7' length of bare copper wire to the top of a doorway. The other end of the wire is looped around a weight, which swings above the floor. I betcha that I can make the weight touch the floor without cutting or disconnecting the wire.

PROPS
    a 10-foot length of bare, 18-gauge, copper wire
    a carpenter's nail
    a hammer
    a 5-lb dumbbell or brick
    an electric hair drier

SETUP
With an adult's permission and help, securely attach the wire to the top of the door frame with the nail: drive the nail into the top of the frame. Wrap the wire around the nail.

    Bend the free end of the wire into a loop around the dumbbell or brick. The weight should be very close to, but not touching the floor.

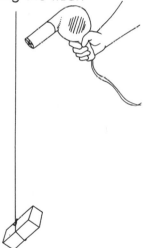

METHOD
Heat the wire with the hair drier. As the wire warms up, it starts to expand in length and the weight will

touch the floor. The coefficient of expansion lets you win this "betcha."

MORE EXPANSION

Pyrex glass is much safer to cook with than regular glass. Glass does not transmit heat easily. When regular glass is heated, heat doesn't travel through it evenly. Some parts become much hotter than others, causing uneven expansion. That partial expansion sets up pressures, called stresses, in the glass that can cause it to break.

Regular glass expands more than twice as much as Pyrex. Because the Pyrex expands less, there are fewer, less powerful stresses. That means that it breaks less easily than regular glass when exposed to heat, and that makes it more useful for cooking, baking, or laboratory use.

A kitchen hint that my grandfather taught me was how to pour boiling hot water, for tea, into a glass. He knew that the hot water could break the glass. Whenever he planned on pouring hot water in a glass to make his tea, he would first place a silver teaspoon in the glass. The reason that the silver spoon kept the glass from cracking is that silver is a very good conductor of heat. The boiling hot water loses a lot of its heat to the spoon. When that happens, less heat stresses are placed upon the glass.

Gramps also knew that using a thick-walled glass would not help. The thicker the glass, the greater the chance that it would break. The thicker the glass, the slower the heat transfers from the inside to the outside, and large stresses are more likely to take place.

"Grandpa's helpful household hint"

Question: When you heat a ring of metal, does the hole in the middle get smaller or larger?

Answer: It gets larger. Imagine a ring of metal wire that is cut in one place and stretched out straight. What happens when you heat it? The piece of wire gets longer. Now imagine that you heat the ring before you cut it. The inside and outside of the ring both increase in length.

One useful thing that comes from knowing about the coefficients of expansion is that it becomes easy to open up a jar with a stubborn twist-off cap. Did you ever try to open up a screw-top jar and couldn't budge the top? What did you do to open it?

Experiment 8
APPARATUS
    1 full factory-sealed, glass jelly jar with screw-on metal lid
      a butter knife
      2 slices of white bread
      a glass of milk

PROCEDURE
First try to open the jar with your bare hands. It's usually pretty tough. Take the jar to your kitchen sink and turn on the hot water. Don't burn yourself. Carefully hold the lid of the jar under the running water and leave it there for fifteen to thirty seconds. Dry the top off and now try to open the jar. It should now open.
    Spread the jelly on one piece of bread and cover it with another slice. Eat the sandwich and drink the milk.

EXPLANATION: When the lid of a jar is heated, it expands at a faster rate than the glass jar, making it a looser fit and easier to unscrew.

Betcha 2
PROPS
    a Ball and Ring set on handles from Morris & Lee (The ball and ring are both brass. The ball's diameter is the same as the ring's inside diameter.

**To open a stubborn jar lid, hold
it under hot running water.**

The ball can just be pushed through the inside of
the ring.)
    a candle

ROUTINE
"I betcha that you can push the ball through the ring,
and that you won't be able to pull it back through for
thirty seconds.

METHOD
Take the ball and ring and push the ball through the
ring. Then heat the ball in the flame of the candle.

Your friend will be unable to pull the ball back through.

EXPLANATION: The ball expands in size when heated and can't be forced through the hole in the ring, unless the hole is also heated, enlarging the inside diameter, or the ball is cooled.

CAUTION: DO NOT TOUCH THE BALL OR RING WITH YOUR FINGERS. YOU WILL GET BURNED. HANDLE THEM ONLY BY THE HANDLES.

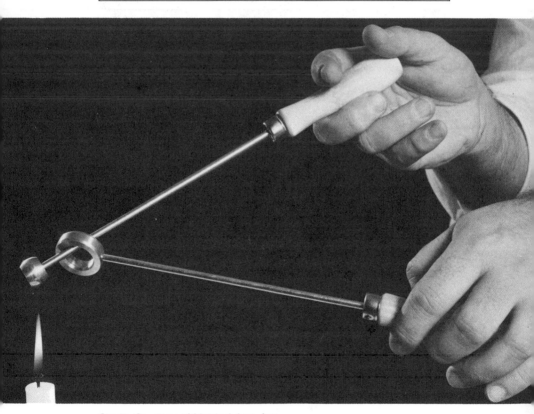

Credit: Courtesy of Morris & Lee, Inc.

BIMETALS

The small amount of expansion of metals, as seen in the Coefficients of Linear Expansion chart, can be enlarged by using a bimetallic strip. A *bimetal* is made up of two different metals with different coefficients of expansion, such as brass and iron, that are welded, riveted, or glued together lengthwise. The different coefficients cause the bimetal strip to bend into a curve when heated or cooled. This exaggerated bending can be useful. Bimetal strips are used inside thermostats that control the heat in your house. When a certain selected temperature is reached, the bimetal strip curves and closes an electrical circuit to turn on your air conditioner in the summer or turn on your heater in the winter.

Bimetals bend when heated.

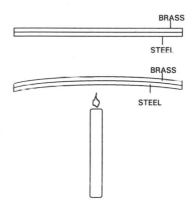

Trick 6
The Mental Push
EFFECT: A pile of coins is placed on a table. You concentrate on the pile and, in a few moments, a few coins move around magically.

PROPS
    a small bunch of coins (twelve or more)
    a jumping disk (available from Edmund Scientific)

ROUTINE

Borrow the coins from your friends, or, if they don't trust you, have some ready in your pocket. Place the coins on the table in a pile. Tell your friends that you will mentally reach over and move some of the coins. Stare at the coins. Make some weird motions in the air with your hands and odd moans with your mouth. In a few moments, your friends will be astounded, for the coins will actually jump about, just as if you mentally pushed them.

METHOD

Without letting your audience in on the secret, prepare the jumping disk. Push the top down until it clicks into place. When you place the coins on the table, make sure that the disk is underneath them, on the bottom of the pile, hidden from everyone's eyes. All you have to do is wait long enough and the disk will live up to its name and jump, causing the coins resting on it to scatter about.

EXPLANATION: The jumping disk is actually a bimetallic disk. When you set it by pushing down the top, you warm it up a little by handling it. It rests in that state until it cools down just a little, and then it returns to its original shape. When it does this, it acts like a spring. It has potential energy that changes into kinetic energy that pushes against the coins, making them jump.

EXPANSION AND CONTRACTION OF LIQUIDS

Liquids generally increase in volume when heated because the molecules move faster and farther apart. The expansion rate for different liquids varies. Alcohol, for instance, expands at a much faster rate than water. Most liquids decrease in volume when cooled, as the molecules move slower and get closer together. Water is one exception to this rule.

Like most other liquids, when cooled enough, water changes physical states and becomes a solid. Unlike most other liquids that decrease in volume when turned into a solid, water actually increases in volume. As water is cooled, it contracts until it reaches 39.2°F. (4°C).

At 4°C, when water is at its densest, it will sink to the bottom of its container. Before any water in the container can freeze, all of it must be at 4°. At that point, its volume starts to increase, and the less dense water floats to the top of the container, until it reaches the freezing point and forms ice.

The specific gravity of water is 1.00. The specific gravity of ice is 0.92.

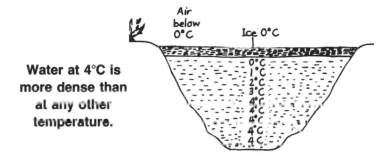

Water at 4°C is more dense than at any other temperature.

Experiment 9
APPARATUS
    an empty, clean, plastic pill bottle
    water
    the freezer section of your refrigerator

PROCEDURE

Fill the bottle with water, and then place it, uncapped, upright in the freezer. When you go back in a few hours, after it's frozen, you'll see the ice coming out of the opening. The ice expanded and moved out of the bottle. If the bottle had been capped, the ice would most likely have burst through the sidewalls of the bottle.

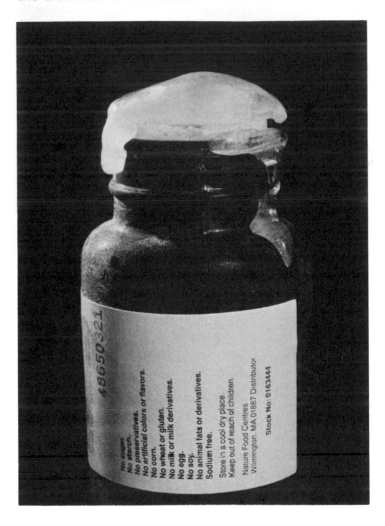

NOTE: Water expansion is the reason that people put antifreeze in their cars, and drain water pipes and swimming pools in the winter. If they didn't, when the water froze, it would wreck lots of things.

Automobile antifreeze is mostly a chemical, called ethylene glycol, that freezes well below 0°C (32°F) and boils well above 100°C (212°F). It is added to the water in the radiator of a car so that the freezing point of the coolant is lowered and the boiling point is raised.

GAS EXPANSION

On page 48 there is a list comparing temperature scales. The one scale that we barely talked about is the *Kelvin scale*. It is also known as the *absolute scale*. It will take a little extra explaining to tell how this scale works, but it's worth it. In this explanation, we're going to use pressure and temperature.

Robert Boyle (1627–1691), a British scientist, discovered that if the temperature remained constant, a gas's volume decreased when the pressure increased, and as the pressure decreased the volume increased.

Jacques Charles (1746–1823), a French scientist, discovered that when you reduced the temperature of any gas by 1 degree Celsius (1⅘ degrees Fahrenheit), the gas decreased in volume by the very small amount of $\frac{1}{273}$ of the original volume.

It worked the other way also. When you raised the temperature by 1 degree Celsius, the volume increased by $\frac{1}{273}$. That also means that if the volume was decreased by $\frac{1}{273}$, the pressure was decreased

by $\frac{1}{273}$. If a gas didn't turn into a liquid or a solid before reaching 273 degrees below the ice point (0 degrees Celsius), the pressure and volume would be reduced to 0. There would be no pressure at all.

In 1848 Lord Kelvin suggested that the volume loss was not as important as the energy loss. This loss affected all matter, not just gases, and would be reached at -273.16 degrees Centigrade (it wasn't called Celsius until 1948). At this point, there would be no movement of any molecules. Kelvin further suggested that a new system of temperature measurement, called the absolute scale, be adopted. Absolute zero would be the starting point, and there would be no negative temperatures. Every degree of temperature in the absolute scale would be equal to a temperature in the Centigrade scale. This means that not only are the temperatures below freezing easy to understand, but so are the highest temperatures in the universe, like those found in the center of stars.

The kinetic theory of heat showed us that molecules were always moving. This movement of gas molecules gives us gas pressure because they push against the walls of the container, smashing into them, changing potential energy into kinetic energy. When we raise the temperature, we add kinetic energy, which means that the molecules hit the walls harder and more frequently, and we end up with

Water molecules move faster and faster when heated.

higher pressure. When we lower the temperature, we take away a little bit of the kinetic energy, which means the molecules don't smash into the walls as hard or as frequently, and we have less pressure.

If we took away all of heat down to zero on the absolute scale, the gas would have zero kinetic energy, wouldn't be pushing on the walls of the container, and would take up zero space. All of this means that absolute zero ($-273°C$) is the lowest possible temperature in our universe. If you were in the "vacuum of space," well beyond the atmosphere of any planet, star, or moon, and you measured the temperature in shadow, you would find a reading of absolute zero.

The temperature in space is absolute 0 when in a shadowed area, away from a heat-radiating surface.

To change from Celsius to Kelvin, you just add 273 to the Celsius number. A temperature of 20 degrees in Celsius is 293 degrees Kelvin.

Trick 7
The Dancing Dime
PROPS
  a dime
  an almost empty glass soda bottle

SET UP
The bottle and coin are on a table in front of you.

ROUTINE
Explain to your audience that you are going to use your highly developed mental powers to make the coin dance. To ensure that you won't use any physical methods such as thread or wires, you will isolate the coin on top of the bottle. Once the coin is directly on top of the bottle, have one spectator grasp the bottle firmly between two hands to hold it steady. In a few moments, the coin starts to dance on top of the bottle, moving up and down with an erratic beat.

METHOD
This trick works by itself. By grasping the bottle, the spectator adds the heat of his or her hands to it. The heat increases the pressure and volume of the air in the bottle. The increased pressure from the air in the bottle pushes up against the dime and makes it move, bouncing it around.

NOTE: It will help this trick a little if the top of the bottle is moist, forming a seal between the coin and bottle.

HEAT CONDUCTION

Have you ever noticed how things that are hot seem to get cool after a while, and that cool things seem to warm up? The reason those two things happen is *conduction.* The kinetic theory of heat says that heat, a form of energy, is the movement of molecules. When you warm something up, you're supplying energy to the molecules, and those molecules move faster.

When two objects are brought next to each other, and one is hotter than the other, the quicker-moving molecules of the hotter object bash into the slower-moving molecules of the cooler object. The

Hot chocolate gets cooler, hand gets warmer.

quicker molecules transfer some of their kinetic energy to the slower ones. Since the warmer, quicker ones lose some energy and the cooler, slower ones gain energy, the warm object loses heat and the cool object gains heat. When they both reach the same temperature, the kinetic energy heat transfer stops. This method of heat movement is called conduction.

Some materials conduct heat very quickly, others very slowly. Metals are usually good conductors, while things like gases, certain plastics, and paper conduct heat slowly. Things that conduct heat slowly are called *insulators.* Wool and goose-down-filled clothing are so warm because there are little pockets of air trapped within the wool fibers and goose down. Since air is a good insulator, very little of your body's heat is conducted through the clothing to the outside.

HOUSEHOLD HEAT TIPS

1. You use a pot holder in the kitchen when a pot's handle is too hot to touch. The handle heated

A pot holder is a good insulator.

up through conduction. The pot holder is a good insulator and keeps the heat from conducting to your hand.

2. You might have seen your mom in a hurry to bake some potatoes. To make them bake faster, there's a very good possibility that she used some aluminum baking nails. She took one and pushed it into the middle of the potato, leaving

the head sticking out. The nail aids the baking because it rapidly conducts heat to the center of the potato, which is much faster than having the heat conducted through the potato itself. Potato is not as good a conductor as the aluminum. The heat will take longer to reach the interior of the "unnailed" potato.

3. Many metal pots and pans have wooden handles because wood is a good insulator and prevents the heat of the pan from being conducted to your hand.

4. Trivets are insulators that allow hot pots, pans, and dishes to sit on a table without burning it.

Betcha 3

DO NOT TRY THIS WITHOUT ADULT SUPERVISION.

I bet that you can boil water with ice in it and the ice won't melt and the water will stay cold.

PROPS
    laboratory test tube
    a small piece of metal wire screen (a patch from a screen door will do)
    tongs with insulated handle
    ice
    cold water
    candle
    matches

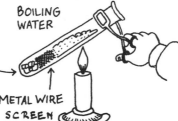

BOILING WATER
ICE →
METAL WIRE SCREEN

SETUP

Chop up the ice and fill ⅓ of the test tube. Place a small piece of screen over the ice, keeping the ice on the bottom. Fill the test tube to within 1 inch of the top with water.

ROUTINE

Light the candle. Hold the test tube in the tongs and let the candle flame play over the water-filled section of the test tube. In a few minutes, the water will boil, but the ice will not melt.

EXPLANATION: The ice doesn't melt for a couple of reasons: 1. Water is a poor conductor of heat. 2. Convection currents do not allow the warm water to sink down to the bottom of the test tube and melt the ice. The warm water is more buoyant than the cold water around the ice and stays at the top of the test tube.

Betcha 4

DO NOT TRY THIS WITHOUT ADULT SUPERVISION.

Three coins are stuck to three pieces of wire by melted wax. The wires are imbedded in a block of wood. Light a candle and say, "I 'betcha' that if you hold the wires over the candle flame, I can tell the order in which the coins will fall off." There is no doubt that you win.

PROPS

3 pieces of stiff wire: iron—from a wire coat hanger; copper—from an electrician's toolbox; aluminum—scrap metal

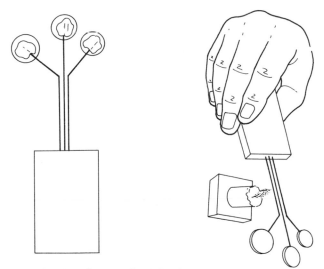

a block of wood, 4-inches square and 1-inch thick

a candle

3 coins—penny, nickel, and dime

SETUP

Drill three holes in 1-inch edge of the block. The holes should be the same size as the wires and next to each other. Bend one end of each wire, as shown in the illustration. Push the other end of the wires into the holes in the block. Melt some candle wax onto each coin and attach one to the end of each wire by letting the wax solidify; put the penny on the copper wire, the nickel on the aluminum wire, and the dime on the iron wire.

METHOD

The wires all conduct heat at a different rate. The copper is the fastest, followed by the aluminum and then the iron. Since the copper conducts heat the fastest, the wax on the penny will melt first, followed by the nickel and then the dime.

Experiment 10
APPARATUS

a clean, smooth tabletop made of plastic or metal

a clean piece of notebook paper, 3 inches square

PROCEDURE

Put the piece of paper on the table. Put your finger on the paper. Rub the paper back and forth quickly while applying pressure with your fingertips. What happens? Why?

You start to feel heat at your fingertips. The molecules of the paper rubbing against the molecules of the tabletop (moving friction) caused an increase in heat. As the molecules moved faster and faster, they started to generate heat.

Experiment 11
APPARATUS

a 10-inch piece of iron wire from a coat hanger.

PROCEDURE

Start to bend the wire back and forth. After a while, it will start to get warm. Be careful. Do it long enough, and you will burn your fingertips.

EXPLANATION: The bending of the wire is mechanical work. By bending the wire to and fro, you are making the molecules of the wire rub against each other. The faster they rub against each other, the faster they start to move. The faster they move, the hotter the wire gets. Heat is caused by the movement of molecules. Eventually, the wire will break from metal fatigue caused by the bending and the friction involved with the bending.

I'm sure that you've heard of rubbing two sticks together (friction) to start a camp fire. When I was a Boy Scout, I learned how to use friction to do this. Here's how.

Experiment 12

```
NOTE: DO THIS OUTDOORS ONLY, WITH
      PROPER ADULT SUPERVISION.
```

APPARATUS

a piece of ½-inch pinewood, 3-inch square, with a ½-inch diameter indentation in the middle of one side

a piece of ½-inch pinewood, 3 inches × 12 inches, with a ½-inch diameter indentation in the middle of one side, and a notch cut all the way through the board, from one edge to the center of the indentation

a 15 inch length of ½ inch hardwood dowel, one end flat, the other end sharpened.

a fire bow (see illustration for construction)

a strong flexible stick

a leather thong

some easily ignitable tinder (dried moss, cotton string, wood shavings, etc.)

NOTE: (a ready-made fire bow may be purchased from Boy Scouts of America supply stores. The stock number is 1527.)

PROCEDURE
Wrap the thong of the fire bow around the dowel one time. Put the long pine piece on the ground with the indentation on the upper side. Place the tinder under the cutout notch. Put the pointed end of the dowel in the indentation. Put the other end of the dowel in the indentation of the second piece of pine. The dowel should now be vertical, one of your hands pressing down on the top piece of pine. Kneel down and place one foot on the bottom piece of pine. With your free hand, start moving the bow back and forth in a sawing motion.

EXPLANATION: The linear (straight line) motion of the bow is transformed into rotary (round) motion by the bow and dowel. As the dowel moves in between the two pieces of pine, the ends start to heat up, due to friction. Continue this for a little while, and you will generate enough heat to ignite the tinder.

The molecules of the dowel rub against the molecules of the pine block. The faster and longer they move, the hotter they get. They eventually get hot enough to start a fire.

HEAT CONVECTION

Have you ever seen a camp fire? The wood burns (stored chemical energy changing into heat energy) and heats the air above it. The warm air rises (according to Archimedes, warm air is less dense and becomes more buoyant), and cooler air from outside of the camp fire streams in, gets heated, and rises, letting more cool air in. As long as the fire is burning, this heating, rising, and replacement of air takes place.

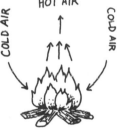

The same kind of thing happens when you put a pot of water on the stove to heat for tea. Cool water replaces hot water in a cycle similar to that of air in the camp fire. This activity of replacing the hot gas

or liquid with cool is called *convection*. Convection is responsible for air currents in the atmosphere. Air is warmed and rises, only to be replaced with cooler air. Convection currents are used to heat homes with hot air heating systems.

In many supermarkets, there are freezers for

storing ice cream that are simply large, open-topped boxes. The warm air, outside of the box, rises so it can't get in the box, and the cold air can't rise over the walls of the box. The construction of the box prevents a convection current from occurring.

There are other types of freezer boxes in a supermarket that are not as energy-efficient as the boxes mentioned above. They are large, upright boxes with front-opening glass doors. If you were to stand in front of one of these boxes when it was opened, you'd feel the cold air rush out over your legs and feet. All of the cold air rushes out, and since it is heavier than warm air, it falls to the floor.

Trick 8
The Power
EFFECT: The person for whom you are doing this trick feels strange waves of power coming from your hands. (There are no props needed for this trick.)

ROUTINE
Ask the person to whom you're doing this trick to hold her hands out in front of her, as though she were praying. Then tell her, "I've been doing magic tricks for years and most of them are tricks. But I've always thought that I've had some strange power that comes from my hands. Let's see if you can feel it."

A spectator feels power emanating from your hands.

Hold your hands just a little lower than her hands, on either side, close but not touching. After your hands are in position, say, "You should be able to feel the power in just a moment, something like a tingling on the back of your hands. Don't be afraid. It can't harm you." In a few moments, she should tell you that she feels something. Say, "I'm glad that you felt that. I will now show you that this power is real." Proceed to do trick 9.

EXPLANATION: This works best on a cool day. The heat coming from your hands sets up a convection current that should go past the back of your helper's hands. That, along with the suggestion that she will feel something, is enough to make this trick work.

Trick 9
The Power Revisited
EFFECT: A piece of paper balanced on a needle starts to turn for no obvious reason.

PROPS
    a cork
    a sewing needle
    a 2-inch square of notebook paper

SETUP
Fold the paper from corner to corner and open it up. Do the same with the other corners.
    Stick the needle into the cork. Balance the center of the paper, where the two folds meet, on top of the needle.

ROUTINE

Refer to the previous trick. "Watch carefully as I cause this piece of paper to rotate without touching it." Put your hands on either side of the paper, one a little closer than the other, without touching it. In just a few moments, a convection current will be set up that starts the paper turning.

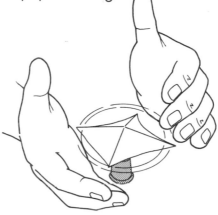

Experiment 13

TO BE DONE ONLY WITH ADULT SUPERVISION

APPARATUS

    kitchen stove
    a pot half full of water
    some rice

PROCEDURE

Place the pot half on, half off the burner. Bring the water to a boil—don't burn yourself. Drop in a few grains of rice. What happens to the rice?

The rice starts moving in a circular path from the top of the water to the bottom and back up to the top again. By placing the pot half on and half off the burner, you have set up warm and cool sections in the pot. A convection current is set up with the warm water rising and the cooler water coming in from the side. The rice is pulled along with this current.

HEAT RADIATION

If you've ever warmed yourself by sitting in front of a camp fire or fireplace on a cool night, you've warmed yourself by heat radiation. You've also experienced heat radiation if you've warmed yourself by sitting in the sun on a cool winter's day or if you've ever used an electric toaster.

With any of those things that are mentioned above, was there any direct contact to transfer heat by conduction? How about by heat transfer by convection? The answer to both questions is no. The cause of the heat—fire, the sun, or glowing wires—sent out waves of radiation. The waves may be visible or invisible, and can travel through empty space.

Most of the energy that we use on earth, excluding nuclear energy, originally came from the sun. The sun's radiation helped plants and animals grow.

Then they died and turned into coal or petroleum. The petroleum and coal power steam and electric generators.

The sun evaporates water that rises into the atmosphere, where it turns into clouds. The clouds eventually turn into rain and the rain falls into lakes and rivers, which flow downhill to the places where people thoughtfully built hydroelectric plants.

Everything radiates heat, even though you may not be able to feel it. If you place your hand next to a cold soda can, both your hand and the soda can send out heat radiation. The reason that your hand feels cool as it nears the can is that the can sends less energy to your hand than your hand sends to the can.

Radiant energy is affected by the color and texture of the warm object. If the object is both dark in color and uneven, it will radiate more heat than if it were lighter in color and smoother. The best radiators of heat are also the best absorbers of heat. The preferred color shades of clothing in warm climates are always light-colored. They absorb less radiant heat.

Experiment 14
APPARATUS
>   2 white paper cups
>   2 thermometers
>   black paint

SETUP
Paint one cup black, inside and out. Punch two small holes in the bottom of each cup. Push the bulb of a thermometer into the interior of each cup, through the hole in the bottom.

PROCEDURE
Note the temperature on the thermometers. They should be equal. Place both cups in a sunny area. Examine the temperature of each cup every 15 minutes. You will find that the temperature of the black

cup rises much more quickly than the temperature of the white cup. The black cup absorbs heat much easier than the white cup.

Betcha 5
Bet your friend that you can cut a string in a sealed bottle without breaking the bottle, removing the string, or using scissors or a knife.

PROPS
    a clear, uncolored, glass soda, ketchup, or milk bottle
    a piece of string
    a small weight like a key or washer
    a cork or cap to go into the mouth of the bottle
    a magnifying glass

SETUP
Tie the weight to one end of the string. Place the weight and string into the bottle. Put the cork or cap on bottle, securing the string so that the weight dangles 1″ from bottle's bottom.

METHOD

Place the bottle in the sunlight. Using the magnifying glass, focus the sunlight into a pinpoint resting on the center of the string inside the bottle. In a few moments, the string will be burned through by the concentrated radiant energy of the sun.

HEAT ENERGY

Mechanical energy can be turned into heat energy by friction. (See Experiment 12.) On the other hand, heat energy can be turned into mechanical work. That's how gasoline, diesel, and steam engines work. Heat is transformed into motion.

You can use a thermometer to find out something about the heat of an object, but there's more to heat than just the temperature. A warm object may have more heat energy than a hot object. A freshly brewed cup of coffee has a higher temperature than a bathtub full of warm water, but the bathtub has a greater total amount of heat energy.

Experiment 15

This is a perfect experiment to run just before you take a bath.

APPARATUS

> 2 trays of ice cubes
> a large kitchen mixing bowl
> a cup of boiling hot water
> a bathtub full of warm water
> a thermometer

PROCEDURE

Find the temperature of the water in the cup and in the tub with the thermometer. Fill the mixing bowl with ice from one ice cube tray. Pour the hot water into the mixing bowl. Put all of the ice cubes from the second tray into the tub of warm water. Compare how fast the ice melts in the cup and in the tub. What happens?

You will find that after a short time the ice in the tub has completely melted while there is still ice left in the bowl. Find and compare with a thermometer the temperature of the water in the cup and in the tub. What do you find?

The temperature of the water in the bowl has dropped to near freezing. The temperature of the water in the tub has barely changed.

EXPLANATION: The amount of heat energy in the tub is much greater than in the cup, even though the initial temperature of the cup's water is greater than the tub's.

CALORIES AND SPECIFIC HEAT

Heat quantity is measured in *calories*. In physics, a calorie is the amount of heat that can raise 1 gram of water 1 degree Celsius. The calorie that people talk about when they try to lose weight is actually a kilocalorie (1,000 calories).

Specific heat is the amount of heat needed to raise 1 gram of a substance 1 degree Celsius. As water is the basis for measuring volume (1,000 grams = 1 liter), it is also the basis for measuring specific heat. The specific heat of water is 1. The smaller the number, the less heat is needed to raise the temperature.

SPECIFIC HEATS

Aluminum	0.22
Brass	0.09
Copper	0.09
Glass	0.2
Ice	0.5
Iron	0.11
Lead	0.03
Mercury	0.03
Silver	0.06
Water	1.00

When a TV repairman has to solder a circuit, he might use a heat sink on an adjoining circuit. A heat sink is a clamp that will conduct heat away from sensitive circuitry that the repairman doesn't want damaged.

Experiment 16

DO THIS ONLY WITH AN ADULT'S PERMISSION AND HELP.

This experiment should be done in your kitchen.

APPARATUS
    kitchen tongs
    a saucepan of water
    a steel ball bearing
    a glass marble
    a block of paraffin wax

(**NOTE:** The ball bearing and the marble should be the same size.)

PROCEDURE
Place the ball bearing and the marble in the water. Bring the water to a boil. Using the tongs, take the ball and marble out of the water and place them away from each other on the block of wax. You will see that the glass marble will melt more wax than the steel ball bearing. The marble has a greater specific heat.

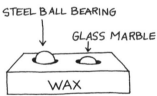

LIQUID TO SOLID

We already know that if we raise the temperature of a solid high enough, we can melt it, turn it into a liquid. We also know that we can lower the temperature of a liquid and turn it into a solid. If we heat a crystalline substance (a substance that forms crystals), the temperature at which it melts is exactly the same as the temperature at which the liquid turns into a solid. For water, a crystalline substance, this temperature is called the ice point, 0° Celsius, 32° Fahrenheit. Objects that are not crystalline—such as solid vegetable shortening, chocolate, and butter—do not have a definite melting point. Chocolate, for instance, gradually melts as the temperature rises. To melt ice, it is necessary to add heat. Soda cools down when we add ice to it. Heat leaves the soda and melts the ice.

Experiment 17
APPARATUS

a cooking/kitchen thermometer—make sure it's clean and that it goes as low as 32°F, if not lower
a glass half filled with your favorite soda
ice cubes
notepad and pencil
2 scoops of vanilla ice cream

PROCEDURE

Put the thermometer in the soda. Note the temperature of the soda. Add ice cubes. Record the temperature of the soda every 30 seconds. You will see that, after a while, the temperature of the soda will stop at about 32° Fahrenheit and will then remain at that temperature as long as ice is in the glass. Adding more ice will not lower the temperature. Once all of the ice is melted in the soda, the temperature will start to climb back toward room temperature.

When you have finished your investigation, you may put the ice cream into the glass and enjoy a well-earned ice cream float.

HEAT OF FUSION AND VAPORIZATION

The amount of heat that is necessary to melt 1 gram of a substance without increasing its temperature is called the *heat of fusion*. Water's heat of fusion is about 80 calories per gram. Energy can not be created or destroyed. Because of this, heat is liberated or given off when water or any liquid solidifies.

An old trick in the colder areas of the country is to place a pan of water under an automobile's engine when parked in a draft-free garage during the winter. The heat given off by the freezing water will help prevent the engine coolant from freezing.

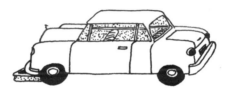

This same concept is sometimes used in the basement vegetable storage areas of a farmhouse. If the temperature falls below freezing, large pots of water may give off enough heat to prevent the water in the vegetables from freezing.

Evaporation is the escape of molecules from a liquid's surface. Only the rapidly moving molecules escape from the cohesive attraction of the others. Because of this, the average speed of all of the molecules in the liquid is reduced. When the average speed is reduced, the temperature falls. Therefore, evaporation drops the temperature, producing a cooling effect.

Experiment 18

APPARATUS
 water

PROCEDURE

Wet your hand and rest it on a table.

Do you feel a cooling effect?

Wet your hand and move it around in big circles.

Do you feel a cooling effect?

Which time did it feel cooler, resting or moving?

When your hand was moving in the air, more water should have evaporated, increasing the cooling effect.

Many mothers will use evaporative cooling when their children are running a fever. Mom will take a cloth, wet it with water, ring it out, and place it on the fevered brow. The evaporation of the water will actually cool the patient down.

The human body works the same way. You probably thought that you sweat so the deodorant companies would have a reason to exist. Not true. Which is not to say that some people don't have GAPO—Gorilla Arm Pit Odor.

The human body sweats as a way of controlling its temperature. As you sweat, water comes out of your pores and covers your skin. The sweat evaporates, cooling the body.

There is a type of air conditioner used in warm, dry climates that cools the air with an evaporative cooling system. Some people call it a "swamp cooler." Water is pumped onto an absorbent material such as cotton. Air is blown through the water-soaked material, evaporating the water and thus cooling the air.

BOILING

We are aware that evaporation takes place at the surface of liquids. When bubbles of vapor form inside the liquid proper, we have boiling. Boiling occurs when the pressure of the vapor equals the pressure of the surrounding air. We can make water boil two ways:

One way is to heat the water, increasing the kinetic motion of the molecules, and causing some of them to break the cohesive bonds and turn into vapor within the liquid. Those are the bubbles that you see inside a pot of boiling water. The bubbles are not volumes of trapped air trying to escape. They are actually water vapor (steam).

If you heat the water, you cannot increase the temperature of the boiling water higher than 100°C (212°F) unless you increase the pressure on the water. Remember, boiling occurs when the pressure of the vapor equals the pressure of the surrounding air. Increase the air pressure, and you can raise the temperature of the water's boiling point. This is the principle behind the pressure cooker found in many kitchens. The pressure is increased and the water gets hotter before it boils. The food cooks that much faster. The same principle is used in many hospital sterilizers to raise the temperature to a point where neither bacteria nor viruses can survive.

Another way to make water boil is to decrease air pressure on the water. When air pressure is less than the sea level value of 14.7 lb/in^2, water will boil at a lower temperature. Many recipes instruct people who live at high altitudes to cook their food for a longer period of time. Water boils at 85° Celsius atop Pike's Peak, Colorado, which is 14,000 feet above sea level. Cooking a 3-minute egg on Pike's Peak may take as long as 5 minutes, because the water is boiling at a lower temperature.

Trick 10
Hot-Blooded
EFFECT: You test a friend to see if he is hot-blooded.

PROP
   a love meter (this is a toy that can be found in novelty and gift shops as well as Edmund Scientific's catalog.)

ROUTINE

Sitting in your favorite fast-food restaurant, you tell your friend that you will test him to see if he is hot-blooded. You have been holding your cold soda up in your left hand. You spring this trick on him just after he's been holding his cold soda cup wrapped in his hand. With your cold left hand, hand him the love meter, instructing him to hold the lower end in the hand that held the soda cup. Tell him to concentrate on hot things, such as cars, bicycles, movies, etc. Not much will happen.

You take the love meter back, holding it in your warm right hand, and show him what a hot-blooded person does to the love meter. The liquid inside of it starts boiling like mad.

EXPLANATION: A liquid with a low evaporation point is placed into the glass envelope and a portion of the air is extracted, causing a partial vacuum to be formed.

When you wrap your warm hand around the lower bulb, the heat from the hand causes a rapid evaporation of the liquid. As the liquid evaporates and turns into a gas, the pressure inside the lower bulb increases and forces the liquid up the tube. The reason why your friend won't make the liquid boil is that his hand is cold from holding the soda cup.

The lower the pressure on a liquid, the lower the temperature necessary to cause rapid evaporation or boiling. Air pressure at the "Mile High City"—Denver, Colorado—is less than air pressure at sea level. People who live in Denver must adjust many of their recipes since water boils at a temperature somewhat less than 100° Celsius because of the lessened pressure.

Trick 11
The Drinking Bird
PROP

a "Drinking Bird" from Johnson Smith Novelty Company

ROUTINE

Inside the bird is a glass tube connected to a glass bulb. The tube and bulb combination is filled with a liquid having a low evaporation point, just like the love meter. The bird's head is covered with fuzz that forms a large area for water evaporation.

The bird is set on a pedestal, enabling it to rock back and forth. The liquid in the bird moves back and forth, from the head to the tail, and changes the bird's center of gravity with its movement. A glass is set in front of the bird's beak and the rocking motion allows the bird to dunk its head into the water. As the water on the fuzzy head evaporates, the fluid condenses and moves toward the tail, starting a rocking motion. Room temperature is enough to evaporate the liquid. The liquid will move up the inner tube, changing the center of gravity of the drinking bird. As long as the proper temperature is maintained and there is enough water, the bird will continue rocking indefinitely. This is not a perpetual motion machine, but a free energy machine that gets its energy from the surroundings.

REGELATION

Regelation is what happens to ice when it is placed under pressure. If the pressure is great enough, the melting point of the ice is lowered. When you ice-skate, the pressure of the blades pushing down on the ice reduces the freezing point of the ice. It reduces it so much that the ice turns to water. As soon as the pressure is relieved, the water reverts back to ice. When you ice-skate, you are really skating on a thin layer of water.

Betcha 6

Bet that you can cut a piece of ice in half without having it fall into two pieces.

PROPS
    a block of ice (freeze water in an aluminum cake pan)
    a thin wire 2 feet long
    2 1-lb weights

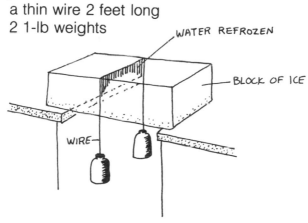

WATER REFROZEN
BLOCK OF ICE
WIRE

SETUP
Place the piece of ice across two supports, like a bridge. Attach one weight to each side of the wire.

METHOD
Lay the wire across the width of the ice. The pressure of the wire will melt the ice directly underneath it. As soon as the wire passes through that point, the water turns back into ice. The wire will pass through the ice in a little while, having cut it in half, but leaving it in one piece just as you said would happen.

WATER VAPOR AND WEATHER

Humidity is the amount of moisture (water vapor) in the air. Condensation (the change from gas into a liquid) of water vapor is called rain. When moist air is cooled, the vapor condenses into a mist or fog of tiny water droplets suspended in air. This is just the

opposite of a foam, which is a gas suspended in a liquid. This mist is called a cloud when it's up in the

sky or a fog when it's near the ground. When the water droplets gather together into large drops, they fall from the sky as rain.

During the winter, when you're outside on a cold day, you can see a fog coming from your mouth. The water vapor in your breath condenses into a fog. During the summer, you can see a fog in a supermarket when you open a freezer case and the dry, cold air meets the warm, moist air.

We talked about sublimation, when a solid transforms directly into a gaseous state. The opposite can also occur: a gas can bypass the liquid state and become a solid. That's how snowflakes are formed in the air. The water vapor solidifies in cold air and becomes that fluffy white stuff. Frost is also formed directly from the gas state. Water vapor in the air solidifies on cold surfaces. Hail is formed when rain falls through cold air, freezing into little chunks of ice

HEAT ENGINES

The law of conservation of energy states that energy can neither be created nor destroyed. What seems to vanish in one form of energy must reappear in another form of energy. Every machine has a certain percentage of wasted energy. The wasted energy doesn't just go into never-never land. That energy is converted into heat energy.

Mechanisms that convert heat energy of a gas to mechanical energy are called *heat engines*. The human body may be considered one such mechanism. Fuel (food) and air are taken into the body and burned to produce heat that is: converted into mechanical work (muscle movement), used for chemical reactions, and used for tissue repair.

Without heat engines, our technology might not have advanced as far as it has. The steam engine was a direct cause of the Industrial Revolution in the early eighteenth century. Gasoline and diesel oil fueled internal combustion engines, and changed the methods of transportation and manufacturing. The jet engine allowed the increase of speeds in air transportation.

EXTERNAL COMBUSTION ENGINES

The steam engine and the nuclear power plant have similarities in the methods of converting heat into mechanical power. They both heat water to the boiling point, usually under pressure. The water then moves a mechanism to convert the heat energy into mechanical or electrical energy.

Originally used in factories to supply energy to power machinery, the steam engine was also used to power construction equipment and railroad locomotives. In this type of machine, water is turned to steam, which enters a cylinder and drives a piston back and forth. This back and forth motion is converted into circular motion through ingenious mechanisms that powered trains all around the world.

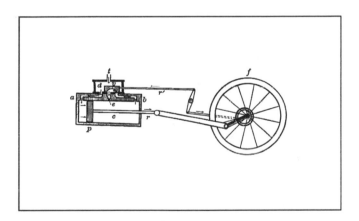

In a nuclear power plant, in a controlled environment, the nuclei (more than one nucleus) of uranium or plutonium atoms split apart and cause a chain reaction, causing other nuclei to split. A by-product of nuclear fission (the splitting of atoms) is heat. The heat generated is used to turn water into steam. The steam is directed against blades of turbines (sort of like propellers). The turbines spin and power electrical generators.

Experiment 19
APPARATUS
   a box of dominoes

PROCEDURE
Stand the dominoes on end in a pattern, as shown in the illustration. The dominoes should be about ½" apart. Push the first domino down so it hits the next one in line. You will see that pushing only one domino started a reaction, knocking all of the others down. This is basically a chain reaction.

The same thing happens inside the core of a nuclear power plant. One atom splits into two or more pieces. Each piece hits a number of atoms that also split, hitting even more atoms. This chain reaction is usually controlled by graphite rods that are inserted into the reactor. The graphite absorbs nuclear particles and prevents the reaction from running amok. When the reaction becomes uncontrollable, there are major problems that affect not only the nuclear plant or the area surrounding the nuclear plant, but the entire world.

INTERNAL COMBUSTION ENGINES

In a two-cycle internal combustion engine, air and fuel enter the combustion chamber from the intake port on the upstroke. When the piston reaches the

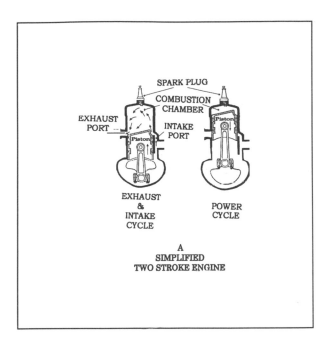

SPARK PLUG

COMBUSTION
CHAMBER

EXHAUST
PORT

INTAKE
PORT

Piston

Piston

EXHAUST
&
INTAKE
CYCLE

POWER
CYCLE

A
SIMPLIFIED
TWO STROKE ENGINE

top of its stroke, the spark plug does its job—gives a spark—and the air/fuel mixture ignites explosively. When the mixture ignites, it turns into a hot gas that expands rapidly, pushing the piston down. As the used mixture goes out of the exhaust port, new mixture comes into the intake port and the pattern repeats itself. These types of engines are found in lawn mowers, snowblowers, snowmobiles, some motorcycles, generators, and small cars.

A four-cycle internal combustion engine is more complex.

Intake stroke: The piston descends and increases the volume of the cylinder, lowering the pressure in the cylinder. As the pressure is lowered, the intake valve opens and the air/fuel mixture enters the cylinder, equalizing the pressure.

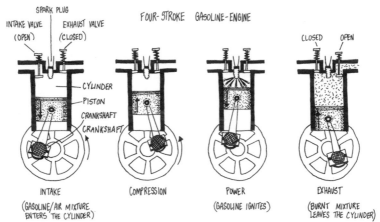

FOUR-STROKE GASOLINE-ENGINE

SPARK PLUG

INTAKE VALVE (OPEN)

EXHAUST VALVE (CLOSED)

CLOSED   OPEN

CYLINDER
PISTON
CRANKSHAFT
CRANKSHAFT

INTAKE
(GASOLINE/AIR MIXTURE
ENTERS THE CYLINDER)

COMPRESSION

POWER
(GASOLINE IGNITES)

EXHAUST
(BURNT MIXTURE
LEAVES THE CYLINDER)

Compression stroke: The intake valve closes as the piston starts to rise, compressing the mixture. As the piston nears the top, the spark plug goes off, igniting the mixture.

Power stroke: The piston descends with the force of the ignited mixture pushing it. As that happens, the piston turns the crankshaft, converting up-and-down motion into rotary motion.

Exhaust stroke: The piston rises and forces out the burned mixture. This type of engine powers planes, automobiles, and some motorcycles.

NOTE: The two-cycle engine gives much more power per stroke, but is much less fuel-efficient. It is not as ecologically sound. It uses lots of gas and puts out lots of pollutants.

JET AND ROCKET ENGINES

The jet engine carries its own fuel and gets air/oxygen from the atmosphere. The rocket carries its own supply of fuel and oxygen. Other than that, the two act in a rather similar manner. The hot gases expand and rush out the rear of the engines. This action has an equal reaction, pushing the engine and whatever it is attached to—plane, rocketship, boat—in the opposite direction.

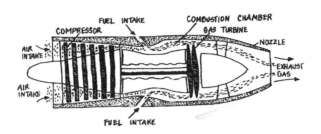

THE REFRIGERATOR

How is the refrigerator in your house like the engine in the family car?

Unlike the engines mentioned above that use heat to make them move, the refrigerator is used to make heat move from one place to another. It takes heat from the inside of an insulated box and moves it to the outside. Refrigerators and air conditioners use fluorocarbon gases, such as freon, as a coolant, as they are easily vaporized and compressed back into liquid, but they have proven to be ecologically dangerous. The fluorocarbon gases attack the protective ozone layer in the stratosphere and allow dangerous amounts of ultraviolet rays to hit the earth's surface. The search for a safer coolant is underway.

The refrigerator is an insulated box. Inside its walls are tiny pipes filled with coolant. The coolant enters the box as a liquid but then evaporates and turns into a gas. As you know, when a liquid evaporates, it becomes a warm gas, drawing the heat away by conduction. The warm gas now leaves the

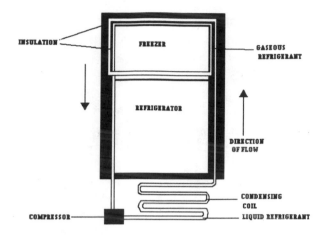

INSULATION

FREEZER

GASEOUS
REFRIGERANT

REFRIGERATOR

DIRECTION
OF FLOW

CONDENSING
COIL

COMPRESSOR

LIQUID REFRIGERANT

insulated box and goes through a pump called a compressor, which puts it under pressure. As the coolant/refrigerant leaves the compressor under high pressure, it enters a condenser, where it gives up heat and turns back into a liquid. It then flows back into the pipes in the walls to start the cycle all over again.

SUPPLIERS

When asking for any of these catalogs, please mention that you saw the company's name in one of Bob Friedhoffer's books.

Johnson Smith Novelty Co.
P.O. Box 25500
Bradenton, Florida 34206-5500

Free catalog from one of the original novelty supply companies in the country

Edmund Scientific Company
101 E. Gloucester Pike
Barrington, New Jersey 08007-1380

Free catalog full of good things for the budding scientist

Morris & Lee Inc.
85 Botsford Place
Buffalo, New York 14216

Send for free catalog of genuine scientific apparatus at great prices

AIN Plastics
300 Park Avenue South
New York, New York 10010

Source for plastic "crystal balls" and fiber-optic rods; drop them a note to ask them about cost and availability

Mickey Hades International
Box 1414
Calgary, Alberta
Canada T2P,2L6

Send for free price list of great selection of magic books from the largest magical publisher

Paul Diamond's Mail Order Magic
P.O. Box 11570
Fort Lauderdale, Florida 33339

Good prices, good tricks, price list—$1.50; mail order only

Zanadu
772 Newark Avenue
Jersey City, New Jersey 07306

$.50 for catalog of exclusive magic effects; mail order only

Louis Tannen Inc.
6 West 32nd St.
New York, New York 10001-3808

Ask to be placed on the free mailing list of one of America's largest magic stores; visit when you're in New York

Hank Lee's Magic Factory
125 Lincoln St.
Boston, Massachusetts 02205

Ask to be placed on the free mailing list of one of America's finest and largest magic stores; visit when you're in Boston

Abbot's Magic Co.
Colon, Michigan 49040

Ask for the cost of the huge catalog filled with goodies

Land of Magic
450 N.E. 20th Street
Boca Raton, Florida 33431

A great retail magic and novelty store; free mail-order catalog for the asking

FOR FURTHER READING

Asimov, Isaac. *Asimov's Chronology of Science and Discovery*. New York: Harper & Row, 1989.

Bobo, J. B. *Coin Magic*. New York: Dover Publications, 1982.

Epstein, Lewis Carroll. *Thinking Physics*. San Francisco: Insight Press, 1979–1988.

Gardner, Martin. *Encyclopedia of Impromptu Magic*. Chicago: Magic Inc., 1978.

Gardner, Robert. *Famous Experiments You Can Do*. New York: Franklin Watts, 1990.

Gonick, Larry. *The Cartoon Guide to Physics*. New York: Harper Perennial, 1991.

Macauly, David. *The Way Things Work*. Boston: Houghton-Mifflin, 1988.

Tarbell, Harlan. *Tarbell Course in Magic, Vols. 1–7*. New York: Louis Tannen.

Walker, Jearl. *The Flying Circus of Physics*. New York: Wiley and Sons, 1977.

INDEX

Page numbers in *italics* indicate illustrations.

Absolute scale, 45–*46*, *48*, 63–*65*

Amontons, Guillaume, 43–44

Archimedes, 75

Atom, *13*

Atomium, *15*

Betcha 1, 52–54, *53*

Betcha 2, 56–*58*

Betcha 3, *69*–70

Betcha 4, 70–*71*

Betcha 5, *82*–83

Betcha 6, *95*–96

Bimetals, *59*–60

Boiling, 90–95, *93, 94*

Boyle, Robert, 63

Brown, Robert, 14–*16*, 18

Brownian motion, 14–16, *17*–19

Calories, 42; and specific heat, 84–86

Capilllary action, 34–36, *35*

Celsius, Anders, 45

Celsius scale, 45, 48; and Kelvin scale, 64–65; thermometer, *45*

Centigrade, 45, 64

Charles, Jacques, 63

Cloud, 96–*97*

Coefficients of linear expansion, *50*

Cohesion, 23; and heat, *24*; of liquids, *29*; in solids, 23. *See also* Surface tension

Convection, 75

Crystalline structure, 19–20

Crystalline substance, 86

Curie, Marie Sklodowska, 9

Dancing Dime (trick), 65–*66*

Democritus, 13, 14

Diving Water (trick), 30–*32*

Drinking Bird (trick), *94*–95

Ductile, defined, 28

Einstein, Albert, 9

Elasticity, *26*

English system, 12

Evaporation, *21*, 88

Experiment 1, 16–17

Experiment 2, 17–18

Experiment 3, *20*–21

Experiment 4, *21*–22

Experiment 5, 25

Experiment 6, 29–*30*

Experiment 7, 35–*36*

Experiment 8, 56, *57*

Experiment 9, 61–63, *62*

Experiment 10, *72*

Experiment 11, *72*–73

Experiment 12, *73*–75, *74*

Experiment 13, 78–79

Experiment 14, *81*–82

Experiment 15, 83–*84*

Experiment 16, 85–*86*

Experiment 17, *87*–88

Experiment 18, *89*–90

Experiment 19, *100*

External combustion engines, *99*–100

Fahrenheit, Daniel Gabriel, 44

Fahrenheit scale, *48*

Fahrenheit thermometer, *44*

Floating Disk (trick), 32–34, *33*

Foam, defined, 96

Fog, defined, 97

Franklin, Rosalind Elsie, 9

Frost, defined, 97

Galilei, Galileo, 9, 42–43

Gas, 22; molecular action of, *22*–23

Gas expansion, *63–66*, 65

Hail, defined, *97*

Hardness, measurement of, 29

Heat, 37–97; effect of on molecular action, 21; kinetic theory of,

Heat (*cont.*)
41–42, 64–65, *67*;
uses of, *37*
Heat conduction, 66–*67*
Heat convection,
75–79, 76, 77, 78
Heat energy, 83–*84*
Heat engines, 98–*99*
Heat of fusion, *88–90,
89*
Heat radiation, *79*–83,
80, 81, 82
Heat sink, 85
Hot-Blooded (trick),
91–*93*
Household heat tips,
67–*69, 68*
Human Thermometer
(trick), 39–41, *40*
Humidity, 96
Hypnotic Flower (trick),
18–20

Internal combustion
engines, 100–*102,
101*

Jet and rocket engines,
102–*103*
Jokes, *39*
Joule, James Prescott,
41–42
Joules, 42
Jumping Rubber Band
(trick), 26–*27*

Kelvin, Lord, 45–46, 64
Kelvin scale, 45–*46, 48,*
63–*65*

Liquids, 21;
characteristics of,
29–34; expansion
and contraction of,
60–63, *61, 62*; to
solid, 86–88, *87*

Malleable, defined, 28
Matter, kinetic theory of,
19–23
Medici, Ferdinand II
de', 43
Mental Push (trick),
59–*60*
Metric system, 12
Mohs' scale, *29*
Molecular action, 19–23
Molecular forces,
23–25
Molecule, *14*; in rapid
motion, 14–16

Nuclear fission, 99

Perelman, Yakov,
49–50
Plasticity, 27–*28*
Power (trick), *76*–77
Power Revisited (trick),
77–78
Pyrex glass, 55

Radiant energy. *See*
Heat Radiation
Rain, *96, 97*
Refrigerator, 103–*104*
Regelation, *95*–96
Rumford, Count von,
41–42

Snowflakes, *97*
Solids, 19;
characteristics of,
26–28; expansion
and contraction of,
49–*58, 52, 57*
Specific heat, *85*;
calories and, 84–86
Steel, *24*
Sublimation, 22, 97
Surface tension, 29–*32,
30*

Temperature, *38*;
everyday measuring
of, 46–49, *47, 48*
Tenacity. *See* Tensile
strength
Tensile strength, *23–25*
Thermometer, history of,
42–*45, 43, 44*
Thomson, William. *See*
Kelvin, Lord

Tricks:
Dancing Dime,
65–*66*
Dividing Water,
30–*32*
Drinking Bird,
94–95
Floating Disk,
32–34, *33*
Hot-Blooded,
91–*93*
Human
Thermometer,
39–41, *40*
Hypnotic Flower,
17–18
Jumping Rubber
Band, 26–*27*
Mental Push,
59–*60*
Power, *76*–77
Power Revisited,
77–78
Turbines, 99–100

Vapor, 21

Water vapor (steam),
91; and weather,
96–97
Weather, water vapor
and, *96–97*